D1123695

Rev Up Your Writing in
Opinion
Pieces

BY LISA M. BOLT SIMONS • ILLUSTRATED BY MERNIE GALLAGHER-COLE

The Child's World®

Published by The Child's World®
1980 Lookout Drive • Mankato, MN 56003-1705
800-599-READ • www.childsworld.com

ACKNOWLEDGMENTS
The Child's World®: Mary Berendes, Publishing Director
Red Line Editorial: Editorial direction and production
The Design Lab: Design

PHOTOGRAPHS ©: Shutterstock Images, 6; iStockphoto,
12; Darrin Henry/Shutterstock Images, 18

ISBN 9781634070669
LCCN 2014959945

Printed in the United States of America
Mankato, MN
July, 2015
PA02261

ABOUT THE AUTHOR

Lisa M. Bolt Simons is a writer and teacher. She has published ten books, with more on the way. Her writing has been recognized with awards and grants, including one to travel to Africa. Originally from Colorado, she lives in Minnesota with her husband and twins. Her Web site is www.lisamboltsimons.com.

ABOUT THE ILLUSTRATOR

Mernie Gallagher-Cole is a children's book illustrator living in West Chester, Pennsylvania. She loves drawing every day. Her illustrations can also be found on greeting cards, puzzles, e-books, and educational apps.

Table of Contents

CHAPTER ONE

An Introduction to Writing Opinion Pieces

Do you have a certain point of view? Do you want to share your thoughts with others? If so, you can write an opinion piece. An **opinion** is what you believe about something. This belief is often based on your experiences. But an opinion is not a **fact**. Some people will probably disagree with your opinions.

An opinion piece is writing that shows your thoughts and ideas about a topic. It tries to reason with the reader. It tries to show that your opinion is right. Sometimes an opinion piece asks for change. Sometimes it offers solutions to a problem. Other times it draws attention to what you believe is a problem.

But an opinion piece does more than share opinions. It also gives **arguments**, or reasons, that support the opinion. These arguments help the reader trust the writer.

Tone is important in opinion pieces. The tone is the style of writing. When writing opinion pieces, the tone depends on your message. For example, suppose a person is attacked by a dog. You want to write an opinion piece about using leashes. The tone of your piece would be serious.

But the tone does not always have to be serious. It can be humorous. For example, suppose the school wants to stop having recess. You want to write about all the fun

In 380 BC, a **philosopher** named Plato wrote about the difference between opinions and knowledge. Opinions can have mistakes, he wrote. That means opinions can be wrong. But knowledge is different, he explained. Knowledge does not have mistakes. So Plato believed knowledge was never incorrect.

things students do at recess. The tone of your piece could be funny.

Whichever tone you choose, keep it the same all through the piece. Also try to stay respectful. Making a reader angry will not help get your ideas across.

When writing an opinion piece, it is important to know the audience. In other words, you must understand who will read the piece. Knowing the answer can help you decide what and how to write.

A good opinion piece uses **active voice**. It includes **declarative sentences**. It also uses linking words to help readers connect one argument to the next. All of this writing leads you to make a point. The point is your opinion.

LET'S CHANGE LUNCH

I'm a fifth grader. I'm taller than a kindergartner. I weigh more than a kindergartner. I'm five years older than a kindergartner. But I get the same serving of lunch as a kindergartner.

In the last couple of years, rules have changed for school lunches. I understand why pepperoni was taken away. It was too salty and too fatty. I understand why more fruits and vegetables were added. That food is good for us. But I don't understand why we fifth graders get the same amount of food as younger students. By the end of the day, my tummy is rumbling.

Kindergartners can't eat much. They throw away a lot of food. Older students could use that food for their bigger bodies.

Each kindergartner and first grader should get half a scoop of fruits and vegetables. Kids in second and third grade should get one scoop. Kids in fourth and fifth grade should get two scoops. For the main dish, give kindergartners half. For example, give them half a sandwich. Give older kids a whole sandwich.

Let's change lunch!

CHAPTER TWO

Audience and Argument

When you write an opinion piece, you must know who will read it. Who will be the audience? This is an important question to answer before you start writing.

Sometimes you write for an audience that agrees with you. This makes your job easier. You do not have to convince anyone that you are right. But you still have to support your opinion. The audience may not have thought of the same arguments you did.

More often, your audience will have both **supporters** and **opponents**. For example, a newspaper has a large audience. That means people with different opinions read it. If you write a letter to the newspaper, some readers will probably agree with you. But others will probably disagree.

Sometimes your audience might completely disagree with you. But do not let that stop you. Just make sure to

Some of the earliest opinion pieces were printed in the 1700s.

note your opponents' views. This helps your readers connect with you. They will see that you understand their arguments. Then you can explain why your arguments are stronger. You might even write that you agree with some of their arguments. This helps gain your opponents' trust and respect.

Having a strong opinion is not enough. You also need to support your opinion using facts. Make sure to find reliable sources. This will make your audience trust you more. For example, suppose you get information from a friend. Your audience may think your opinion is unreliable. Now suppose you get information from an expert. Your audience is more likely to trust you.

VOTE YES FOR UNIFORMS

In a few weeks, our city will vote about school uniforms. Some people want them. Some do not. I am a student who wants school uniforms.

We have a lot of poverty in our city. In fact, 65 percent of the students live in poverty. Families barely have enough money to buy food and clothes.

I understand what the opponents are saying. Yes, the same colors can be boring. Yes, students will look similar. But uniforms have a lot of advantages for students and their families.

Uniforms are more affordable than other clothes. So parents will spend less money. And parents only have to worry about three colors. These colors can be mixed and matched many ways. Students will not have to spend much time picking out clothes.

Uniforms mean unity. They show that we are one school. Uniforms mean equality. No more designer versus secondhand clothes. Uniforms mean safety. Teachers know that all the students are dressed the same. This way, they can spot people who do not belong in the school.

When it's time to vote, please vote yes for uniforms.

QUESTION

Who is the audience for this opinion piece? Find one example of a fact the writer uses to support the opinion.

CHAPTER THREE

Getting to the Point

You have a reason to write an opinion piece. Something made you want to share your thoughts. But your piece should not be about everything that you care about. Pick one issue and make your point. State your opinion early in the piece. This can even happen in your first sentence.

You want people to pay attention to your piece. Be sure to use strong **verbs**. Compare these two sentences:

The computer <u>was broken</u> by the girl.

The girl <u>broke</u> the computer.

The first sentence is passive. It uses the verb *was broken*. The second sentence is active. It uses the verb *broke*. Active verbs are stronger than passive verbs. They make an opinion piece more interesting.

Another way to make your pieces stronger is by using declarative sentences. These sentences give ideas. They make comments. They do not ask questions. But

Active verbs help the reader understand who is doing the action. Active verbs also create stronger images in the reader's mind. For example, *eat* and *write* are more interesting verbs than *was* and *were*.

sometimes they may answer opponents' questions. This helps readers see that you understand the topic.

Keep your declarative sentences short. This will make your piece easier to understand. Also, be sure to use linking words and phrases. Examples include *because*, *therefore*, *since*, and *for example*. These words can help you organize your supporting arguments.

People are busy. They do not have time to read lots of pages. Opinion pieces in the newspaper may have only 350 words. They rarely have more than 750. This length is good even if you do not plan to publish your piece. It is best to have a short piece that makes your point. Readers may stop paying attention if your piece is too long.

Now go write your opinion piece. Make your voice heard!

NO TO EXTRA DEVICES

I'm a third grader, and I say no to electronic devices for all students. No, I'm not crazy.

Lots of schools today give students electronic devices. Some are small tablets. Some are laptops. Students use these devices at school. But they also take the devices home.

Our school plans to give devices to all students. I don't like this idea for several reasons. One, most students have devices at home. They do not need the extra device. The school can help families that cannot afford a device. Two, not enough young students are responsible. They will break or lose the devices. Three, students are getting too much "screen time." In other words, students use computers too much as it is. They always look at screens instead of books, planners, or their friends. If we are not careful, our faces will get flat and we will grow cords out of our back pockets!

QUESTIONS

Can you find an example of a declarative sentence with an active verb? What is the tone of this opinion piece?

TIPS FOR YOUNG WRITERS

1. Opinion pieces are just one kind of writing. Young writers should write in lots of different styles. Write fiction. Write fact. Write anything.

2. Read letters to the editor in your local paper. Do you agree with the writers? Why or why not?

3. Write an opinion piece that is serious. Now try to write about the same topic in a funny way.

4. Think about an issue you feel is important. Write an opinion piece. Have an adult read it over. Send it to the local newspaper to see if it will get published.

5. Find an opinion piece in the local newspaper. Now try writing an opinion piece that supports the opposite view.

6. Change sentences written in passive voice to active voice.

7. Read an opinion piece. Then read a news article. What makes these different?

8. Write an opinion piece in a very angry voice. Then write it again in a much calmer voice. Read them aloud. Which one do you think would reach the audience the best? Why?

GLOSSARY

active voice *(AK-tiv vois):* Active voice is when the subject of the sentence does something. *The dog wags its tail* is a sentence that uses active voice.

arguments *(AR-gyu-ments):* Arguments are reasons that support an opinion. The boy had many arguments to support his opinion about using dog leashes.

declarative sentences *(de-KLAR-uh-tiv SEN-tens-ez):* Declarative sentences tell ideas, not ask questions. *It is hot outside* is a declarative sentence.

fact *(FAKT):* A fact is something that is real or true. Saying that George Washington was the first U.S. president is a fact because people can prove that it is true.

opinion *(o-PIN-yun):* An opinion is what a person thinks about something. Saying that chocolate is the best ice cream flavor is an opinion because not everyone agrees that it is true.

opponents *(uh-PON-ents):* Opponents are people who do not agree with a person or idea. The mayor's opponents say she is doing a bad job.

philosopher *(fi-LOS-uh-fer):* A philosopher is a scholar or a thinker. Plato and Socrates are famous philosophers from ancient Greece.

supporters *(suh-POR-ters):* Supporters are people who agree with a person or idea. The mayor's supporters say she is doing a great job.

tone *(TOHN):* Tone is the style or manner in writing. The author used a serious tone when writing about lost dogs.

verbs *(VURBS):* Verbs are words that show action. In the sentence *Elisabeth reads every night*, the verb is *reads*.

TO LEARN MORE

BOOKS

Harper, Leslie. *How to Write an Op-Ed Piece*. New York: Rosen Publishing Group, 2014.

Howell, Sara. *How to Write an Opinion Piece*. New York: Rosen Publishing Group, 2014.

Proudfit, Benjamin. *Writing Opinion Papers*. New York: Gareth Stevens Publishing, 2014.

ON THE WEB

Visit our Web site for lots of links about opinion pieces:
www.childsworld.com/links

Note to Parents, Teachers, and Librarians: We routinely check our Web links to make sure they're safe, active sites—so encourage your readers to check them out!

INDEX